D1575697

NEW
PATIENTS
NOW

NEW PATIENTS NOW

REGAIN CONTROL OF YOUR PRACTICE
AND DOUBLE YOUR PROFITS

JAY M. GEIER

OWNER AND CEO, SCHEDULING INSTITUTE

Published by Advantage, Charleston, South Carolina.
Member of Advantage Media Group.

ADVANTAGE is a registered trademark, and the Advantage colophon is a trademark of Advantage Media Group, Inc.

Printed in the United States of America.

10 9 8 7 6 5 4 3 2 1

ISBN: 978-1-59932-908-6
LCCN: 2017955919

Some names have been changed to protect the privacy of certain individuals.

Cover and layout design by George Stevens.

This publication is designed to provide accurate and authoritative information in regard to the subject matter covered. It is sold with the understanding that the publisher is not engaged in rendering legal, accounting, or other professional services. If legal advice or other expert assistance is required, the services of a competent professional person should be sought.

Advantage Media Group is proud to be a part of the Tree Neutral® program. Tree Neutral offsets the number of trees consumed in the production and printing of this book by taking proactive steps such as planting trees in direct proportion to the number of trees used to print books. To learn more about Tree Neutral, please visit **www.treeneutral.com.**

Advantage Media Group is a publisher of business, self-improvement, and professional development books. We help entrepreneurs, business leaders, and professionals share their Stories, Passion, and Knowledge to help others Learn & Grow. Do you have a manuscript or book idea that you would like us to consider for publishing? Please visit **advantagefamily.com** or call **1.866.775.1696.**

Thank you to all of the clients who took a risk to do things differently and have shared your amazing journey with us. And to my team: thank you for all of your help to change the lives of so many doctors, team members, and everyone that interacts with them.

TABLE OF CONTENTS

INTRODUCTION

BUSY VERSUS PROFITABLE

As a health practitioner, you're busy. From the minute you walk into your business in the morning, someone wants something from you. You're good at what you do, and you work hard all day long. There's just one problem.

"Busy" doesn't mean "profitable."

Even though you're constantly in demand, you wouldn't know it from the return you're getting on your effort. You're caught up in the urgency of dealing with your patients' needs, and those take precedence over developing a business strategy. You just don't have time to think about acquiring new patients.

As a result, your practice is clearly struggling. And so are you.

You're overwhelmed and confused about how to make it all work. You're under financial stress, maybe even to the point of depending on lines of credit to make payroll. *Maybe I just need to invest in more equipment,* you think to yourself. *Maybe that will miraculously transform the business.* But if you're being honest, you know that that's not true.

The truth is you don't feel that you have control over what it takes to make your business profitable. If anything, the demands of the business are in control of you—you're not the one giving it direction with intentional time, energy, and effort. How can you? You don't have time, energy, or effort to spare.

Most unsuccessful businesses are run by very busy people, and you've learned that firsthand. When it comes down to it, you're just not pulling in enough revenue. And you're ready to disembark from this hamster wheel.

FOCUS SHIFT

What you need is a focus shift.

Up to this point, your focus has been on the external areas of your business: your team, your patients, and the distractions they create. You've been stressing out about things that are beyond your control.

Instead, you need to focus on what you have the ability to change.

Regardless of your age, geographic location, and practice type, you have the power to do things differently. And when you change for the better, your practice changes with you. When you're intentional with your time and energy, you bring in more revenue and are less stressed about finances, and the frustration and overwhelmed feelings disappear because you're not out of control anymore.

That's when you have something that you can work with.

This book is designed to show you how any medical or dental practice can increase its number of new patients in ninety days or less. And that's only the beginning. When you really commit to building your practice intentionally—rather than letting it control you—you will accomplish things you never dreamed were possible.

THE DOCTOR OF DOCTORS

In a way, I am the doctor of doctors and dental practitioners.

I'm the founder of the Scheduling Institute, which has helped more doctors and dentists transform their practices into thriving businesses than any other company in the world. But arriving at a place where I had the knowledge and conviction to serve others was the journey of a lifetime.

I've owned a corporation of some kind since age eighteen, when I launched a board game for school systems called "Drugs/Alcohol: Play It Straight." When I started out, I was driven by money—all I really wanted was to be rich. Not much else really mattered; as long as I was rich, I figured I'd be happy.

Then, at twenty-one, two things happened: I was diagnosed with testicular cancer, and I realized that I was broke.

My view of life changed pretty quickly.

It took a year of intensive chemotherapy to cure the cancer, and those were the worst days of my life—physically and emotionally. But when I pulled out of that, I was a different person. I had stronger faith and a deeper sense of human value. I felt like I had a second chance—and I needed to do something of significance with it.

I went to work in the health care industry. There, my focus shifted from getting rich to the idea of serving people. I realized that the same talented doctors who cured people like me of cancer had a problem of their own: They couldn't reach as many people as they were capable of helping. Meanwhile, my talent was getting new patients through the door. I put it to use bringing to doctors the patients who needed their expertise.

Before long, I started to see the impact I was having. Not only were the doctors happier, their team was happier, the patients were happier—and ultimately that trickles down to the family members and friends of all of those people being affected in a positive way through them.

I recognized that the value I was bringing to the table was much greater than just new-patient generation. I was helping people change their lives—and the lives of others—for the better. And at the same time, the more I focused on genuinely serving others, the more money I made.

It didn't take me long to realize that the same techniques that brought patients to those doctors could bring patients to dentists as well. I knew that by working for others in health care, I could help more people than my job description at the time allowed.

That's when the Scheduling Institute was born.

THE SCHEDULING INSTITUTE

I founded the Scheduling Institute in 1997 as a vehicle to help me make the biggest difference I possibly could in the lives of doctors worldwide.

I personally have more than thirty years of experience running businesses. I have owned and operated more than ten different corporations. As an international speaker, I've connected with tens of thousands of people in the industry through my talks.

The Scheduling Institute has been the leading business in its niche for over a decade. Medical practitioners all over the world seek our advice. Our programs are used in more than ten thousand different offices in several countries. Front-desk team members often add "Scheduling Institute

Certified" to their resumes when looking for a new job—we created that standard through our certification program. Our clients commonly see a 50 to 100 percent increase in new patients just by following the process in this book.

Ten thousand people come to the Scheduling Institute's events each year. We operate the largest staff training university in the world, with more than six thousand active participants enrolled at any given time at our convenient training facilities in Atlanta and Phoenix. The Scheduling Institute is one of the top ten fastest-growing companies in the state of Georgia, and we've been rated the top practice advisory firm by *Dentaltown Magazine* since 2010. We've also won *Orthotown's* Townie Choice Award, which is voted on by industry-leading doctors and practice owners, and been on the *Atlanta Business Chronicle's* Best Places to Work list since 2013.

Every day, the Scheduling Institute creates tremendous value in people's lives. Through this book, it's about to do the same for yours.

TURN THE PAGE

This book is the beginning of a journey.

You're setting out on the road to take back your practice. That venture starts with patient intake. In the chapters ahead, you will learn the complete framework for increasing your new-patient numbers with something as simple as answering the phone correctly. Read this book cover to cover to get a clear grasp of how this process works in theory.

Then, take action. Turn the theory into practice. If you find that that's easier said than done, don't give up and walk away. Leverage the Scheduling Institute to get the support and accountability you need to reach your goals. Some people leave us with a lot of good ideas and never implement a single one of them. But you can take the information you learn here, actually implement it, and reap the rewards of taking that risk. We teach you to do things differently than everyone else in your industry so that you stand out.

And once your patient intake is through the roof, don't stop there. In the final chapter, I'll give you an overview of the steps you can take to keep pushing your business to unimaginable heights, so you can reach beyond this book to the next horizon of success.

Your future is waiting. The knock of opportunity is here. You just have to answer the door.

YOUR NEW STORY

I've crossed paths with thousands of people exactly like you. When they have the desire to change things and make the effort to implement the process I'm about to show you, they don't fail. I've seen unimaginable turnarounds—and that's something I want for you.

Everyone has a story, and you're in charge of your own. You are the common denominator in all your failures, just like you're the common denominator in all your successes. If you want to keep living the same story, you'll do just that. If you're ready to change it, you'll do that, too.

The decision rests with you.

There is an enormous amount of business available out there, and you have what it takes to pick it up. Never talk yourself out of discovering your true capabilities. You can transform your practice from a business that's just scraping by to one that thrives. That begins by taking back control of your employees, processes, and focus, and it culminates in taking control of not only your business but your entire life.

CHAPTER 1

THE NEW MARKET: PATIENT-CENTRIC

I n my early years building the Scheduling Institute, I worked primarily with dentists. As I interviewed them, I asked each one the same question: "What are your specific hours?" Then I compared their answers to a grid I had created that listed when people expected their dental office to be available.

For dentist after dentist, I discovered the same thing. The number of hours during which their front desks answered the phone was only about 50 percent of what their patients expected. Worst of all, the dentists themselves stubbornly insisted that this data had nothing to do with their lack of new patients.

One dentist in particular got under my skin. Dr. Adam Wilson was a talented, good-looking man who practiced in Georgia. John hired me as a consultant to help him build his business. Then he flatly refused to listen to me when I told him that his front desk needed to answer the phones five days a week instead of three. After forty-eight hours of gridlock, the situation came to a head.

"Look, Adam," I said. "You can't keep going on this way if you want to improve. You need to answer your phones 100 percent of the time."

Adam just looked straight at me and said, "Jay, there is just no way that idea is going to work."

Now, when someone tells me that something can't be done, I take it as a personal challenge. I knew I was right, but back then I had no proof. So I made a bet with Adam. "I'll tell you what," I said. "You let my team answer your phone the two days of the week you're not here. Every time I get you a new patient, you have to pay me $100."

He literally laughed at me. "Absolutely," Adam agreed. "We'll do it."

So I set up my own answering service. My team started taking the calls that Adam was missing on those two days when he wasn't answering his own phone.

One month later, Adam had to pay me $700 for the seven new patients I brought in. Those patients were worth about $2,000 apiece. Still, Adam wasn't very happy about my fee.

This went on for six or seven months. I consistently brought in a monthly minimum of seven new patients, and Adam kept shelling out $700 or more for them. Then, quietly, he finally hired someone to answer the phones in his office, because it was cheaper.

Adam never did admit that he was wrong, but that really didn't matter. What really mattered was that he understood what I was trying to explain and that, finally, he implemented the changes needed to capture all those missed opportunities.

THE POWER OF "PATIENT-CENTRIC"

Adam's story is not unique. It applies to almost every medical and dental practice I encounter. Even now, you may be reading this and wondering, *How can something as basic as answering the phone have such a huge impact on my business?*

The answer is simple. It works because it's patient-centric.

"Patient-centric" is the concept of engineering 100 percent of your practice around the convenience of your patients, instead of engineering it around you and your team. It sounds complicated, but in some ways it is actually incredibly simple—even as simple as answering a phone.

When you make the shift to a patient-centric process, you see the results right away. You bring in more new patients, those patients are happy with the service you provide, they refer their friends, and your business thrives. You keep pace with the demands of the market, which leads to enormous success.

On the other hand, if you insist on putting your personal convenience over that of your patients, you won't last long. Your patients will go somewhere else, and you just won't be able to make a profit. Sooner than you think, your business will be gone.

You may think of yourself as being patient-centric already, but most medical practitioners are much less focused on putting the patient first than they think. They just don't realize how *unavailable* they actually are. For example, maybe your answering machine takes messages for you all day. Maybe you always take an hour and a half for lunch. Or maybe you take Tuesday mornings off—along with Wednesdays and Fridays.

These situations happen over and over, and it's hurting your business more than you know. You're not patient-centric if you can't figure out a way to get your phone answered by a live person on a Friday. Instead, you're living under the unrealistic assumption that you're so good and powerful that the patients whose calls you're missing—the ones who don't leave messages on an answering machine—will take the time to call back later. But they're not doing that.

What they're doing is calling other providers.

The shift toward convenience in the accepted health care paradigm is happening whether you choose to adapt to it or not. But when did the patient-centric model become so important? And why is the business side of your practice just as important to your success as your clinical training?

THE NEW FAST-AND-EASY PARADIGM

When I began working with clients, the model of success for a doctor was somebody who worked three days per week. If you could work three days and still be financially successful, you'd made it. It was like a badge of honor.

Just a few decades ago, that business model worked—at the time, people's acceptance of what they thought was required to see a doctor was in its favor. Seeing the doctor was something that you had to do, and other options weren't available. So you just put up with the inconvenience.

Then, the Internet began to take hold. And the world changed.

Suddenly, everything started to revolve around two principles: "fast" and "easy." The rise of the Internet gave us fast-and-easy access to information. Shopping became as easy as a click of a mouse. FedEx delivered packages to our doors overnight. Netflix wiped out Blockbuster by offering the same entertainment in a faster, easier way.

The medical profession was a relative latecomer to the innovation game. But as other industries figured out ways to make everything from meals to phone calls to oil changes happen faster and easier, people realized that they wanted that kind of convenience everywhere—including the doctor's office.

Today, your patients no longer feel like they should have to work around your schedule. They want you to accommodate theirs, five or six or seven days a week. They expect a live person to answer your phone from 8:30 to 5:30, Monday through Friday—at minimum. Employed people want to come in early or late. They want to come in or call during the evenings and on Saturdays.

The shift that the rest of the market has already made is finally reaching the health care field. Your patients will not wait around for you, specifically. They will go wherever it's easy.

And that means you need to engineer a practice that's easy to do business with.

THE GREAT MISCONCEPTION: BUSINESS VERSUS TRAINING

A practice that's easy to do business with is one that takes its business side seriously.

The great misconception is that expanding your clinical knowledge will translate into a more successful business. It's true that there is a correlation between the two. However, the specialized knowledge of patient acquisition is unquestionably more profitable than advancing your technical training.

For example, most universities are full of extremely knowledgeable—yet broke—professors. The same is true of medical and dental practices: There are many highly skilled medical practitioners whose practices barely produce enough income to break even.

You aren't taught how to run the business side of your practice during your clinical education. That's not surprising, because the people who teach at universities are typically not successful clinicians or businesspeople themselves. They don't know *what* to teach you, so of course there are few, if any, business courses for doctors and dentists.

You need to get that education for yourself. You need to balance the scales between business and clinical training.

The more you apply business principles to your practice, the more successful you'll be. Your clinical training is important, but it's not the core of the issue. Other people out there can do what you do. Today, what makes a practice stand out is not the provider's capabilities—it's the delivery of the service.

What are your hours of availability? How easy is it to schedule an appointment to be seen? How many different services do you offer under one roof? Can your patients get everything done in one stop instead of hopping from office to office?

How often does a live person answer the phone?

THE INTAKE REVOLUTION

The old model of running health care practices is fast becoming an endangered species. That's not a reason to panic, but it is a good reason to flip the old model around and unwind your incorrect assumptions about how to build a successful business. The evolution involves your intake process and the five key steps you need to take to increase your new patients.

Change Your Mindset: Commit. Before you can change the rest of your business for the better, you as its leader need to have your head in the right place. I'll show you the mental shift that needs to occur within yourself if you truly want to develop a great practice.

Create Your Baseline. You need to know where you are before you can figure out where you're going. To do that, you have to understand your average patient intake and set a realistic baseline of improvement for your office based on where you are right now.

Train Your Team. Most doctors completely under-train their team yet have very high expectations of what those team members should be able to accomplish. I'll explain how to train and incentivize your staff correctly, so that they can bring exponentially more value to the table.

Set Goals. Once you have your system in place, you need to make the most of it by spelling out exactly where you want it to take you. Some doctors actually set goals that work against them. I'll show you how to use goal-setting the right way to maximize your success.

Track Your Progress and Get Accountability. Lack of accountability is the single biggest problem that derails implementing a new, better intake process. Not only must the progress of your team be tracked, but you must also hold yourself accountable. The specific accountability guidelines I'll share with you will teach you how to make that happen.

Just by overhauling your intake process, you will see incredible results in your new-patient numbers. But getting new patients through the door is only the start of a much larger journey. In the final chapter, I'll outline the rest of this road for you so that you understand how to keep growing and moving forward to the next horizon of success.

You have the ability to deliver high-volume, high-touch, high-speed, and high-quality service to your patients. All you have to do is leverage this ability to your advantage to create the practice—and the life—you really want.

The process I'm about to teach you isn't rocket science. It all starts by modifying what happens with the first phone call to your office. This, on its own, can dramatically change the

GEIER

number of new patients who walk through your door. Then stick to the same guidelines that have worked for thousands of doctors before you, which begin with the first step: changing your mindset.

18

CHAPTER 2

CHANGE YOUR MINDSET: COMMIT

'm often approached by doctors about their issues after they hear me speak. One encounter in particular really jumpstarted a doctor into making the choice to change his mindset—and that made all the difference.

I had just come off stage from giving a speech about how to double your practice at one of the Scheduling Institute's Customer Appreciation Events when a man walked up to me.

"You know, I really enjoyed the day," he said, after introducing himself as Dr. Fred Jones from Florida. "But I have to tell you, my practice is different."

"Okay. Tell me what's different about your practice," I replied.

"Well," Fred explained, "it's different because I'm going through a divorce. I don't want my practice to be too successful because then I'll have to pay my wife more money."

I looked at him for a second. Then I said, "All right. Would you like me to tell you what you want to hear, or would you like me to tell you the truth?"

Fred chose the truth.

"I think you're absolutely ridiculous," I told him bluntly. "What you just told me is an excuse. You and your wife don't like each other, so now you're going to spend the rest of your life trying to figure out how not to pay her? Don't you think that's going to have severe consequences on your practice, not to mention the rest of your life?

"I think you need to grow up," I went on as Fred stood there staring at me. "What you need to do is grow your practice so aggressively that you can write that stupid check to your wife and it doesn't even bother you, no matter how much you're giving her. That's my advice, and you can take it or leave it."

Fred mumbled something and sheepishly walked away. I went back to talking to clients.

Six months later, that same man came up to me at another event.

"You know, I've got to be honest with you," he said, "I was really pissed off at you that day at the Customer Appreciation Event. You're the only person who's said anything like that to me, ever. But when I went home, I couldn't get it out of my head. I realized you were right: I was obsessed about not having to pay her. So I've decided to put that excuse aside. I'm going to follow your advice."

Fred changed his mindset that day. Two years later, he had tripled the size of his practice.

Although this is just one example, everyone has an excuse they see as valid.

MIND BEFORE MATTER

I mentioned in the introduction that a big part of taking back your practice is focusing on the things you can control. The first thing you have control over is the way you think.

Your mindset has a huge impact on your business. Why? Because everything in your office is a reflection of you. You may think that what goes on in your head is your own business, but that's not the case. You're the leader of a small office environment. When everyone around you follows your attitude and behavior, your thoughts don't end in your head—they become your company culture.

That puts an enormous amount of power in your hands, which can be a good thing or a bad thing. If you get your mindset right, you will see a positive impact on your practice right away. The excuses will disappear, and the new ideas you implement will yield great results. But if you jump straight to the ideas without dealing with your mindset first, it's like pitching a ball to someone who doesn't have a bat to hit it with. The ideas just will not fly, even if they're good ones.

If you just want everything and everyone around you to change without putting in the work to change yourself, you may as well stop reading right here. But if you invest the time and effort into developing a strong personal mindset, you will enable yourself to use the powerful tools I'll be sharing with you in the next few chapters.

The willingness to make the mental transformation to a fully responsible, patient-centric practitioner is a big struggle for every doctor. A lot of times, your old mindset is in direct conflict with becoming patient-centric. But even though this shift starts with you, you have to remember that it's about more than you alone. It's about teaching your business to become a business.

In this chapter, I'll walk you through the five shifts to a patient-centric mindset: take responsibility, become a "yes" office, abandon the "something for nothing" attitude, accept that business needs to play a role in your practice, and ensure that business and personal views don't mix.

SHIFT 1: TAKE RESPONSIBILITY

The first mindset shift required for any great transformation is to take full responsibility for yourself by eliminating excuses from your life.

Excuse-making is more rampant than most of us are aware of. When things aren't getting done the way we want them to, we tend to revert to excuses. The problem with constantly making excuses is that you literally begin to feel like you have no control over anything. You get the idea that circumstances and other people are in charge of your outcomes.

That just isn't true. You are always in full control of you. And when you understand that, you can do really well regardless of circumstances. What you have right now is what you deserve to have. If you only have ten new patients, then that's all you've been responsible for. If you want that number to go up, you have to trade in more excuses for greater responsibility.

Nobody thinks they have excuses. They think they have special circumstances. But here's the truth: special circumstances are nothing but excuses, just like Fred's divorce from his wife was his excuse not to grow his practice. Marriages going bad, lifestyles unexpectedly changing—everyone is dealing with something outside their norm. But those occurrences aren't valid reasons not to take responsibility for your business and your life.

Your no-excuses mindset has to stretch across all aspects of your life. You should have no excuses when it comes to your family, no excuses when it comes to your patients—no excuses for anything at all. As soon as excuse-making invades any one piece of your life, it bleeds into all the others.

Creating a no-tolerance zone for excuses can be a much more difficult mindset shift than you think. But when you get it right, it will have a major impact on your practice.

SHIFT 2: BECOME A "YES" OFFICE

The next mindset shift you must make is to approach your practice as a "yes" office.

A "yes" office is a practice where the answer to pretty much anything a patient asks is "Yes, we can do that"—as long as it doesn't challenge you legally or morally. The goal with this shift is to eliminate the word "no" from your interactions with patients.

That goes back to being patient-centric. Maybe you and your staff have been focused on your personal convenience up to this point. Maybe you have protocols in place that generate automatic "nos" to some of the questions your patients ask you. Someone asks if you take such-and-such insurance, and your answer is, "No, we don't." End of conversation.

When you make this mindset shift, you do everything in your power to turn that "no" into a "yes." "Yes," you say, "we take every insurance, and we'll work with you to resolve any insurance issues you have." Whenever the patient asks for something, say "yes." Then develop a creative way to make that "yes" happen.

Q: Can I come in at 5 p.m.?

A: Yes, we do offer 5 p.m. appointments on Thursdays.

Q: Do you offer Zoom whitening?

A: We offer an in-office whitening that patients say is gentler on their teeth.

Cultivating a "yes" office mindset doesn't just increase your new-patient intake. It leads you to a wealth of profitable business opportunities you never would have discovered otherwise.

SHIFT 3: ABANDON "SOMETHING FOR NOTHING"

The third mindset shift you must make is abandoning the mentality of wanting something for nothing.

Wanting something for nothing is one of the worst attitudes you can have when you're working to grow your practice. You want new patients, but you don't want to do anything to get them. You want a great team, but you want all your systems and processes to stay the same. You want a successful business, but you don't want to look at your checkbook. Being cheap is a variation of wanting something for nothing.

That is a recurring theme and a big struggle for many doctors. But business just isn't compatible with the concept of getting something for nothing. If you want everything for free, that's the kind of patient you will attract. If you want patients who are willing to pay for great service, you have to behave as if that's what you offer—great service at a great value.

The truth is that if you want to be rich, you have to over-deliver in service value. The more you put into your practice, the more you're going to get out of it. That's the formula for success.

SHIFT 4: ACCEPT THAT BUSINESS NEEDS TO PLAY A ROLE

The fourth shift to your mindset is the acceptance that business needs to play a role in your practice.

I touched on this in the first chapter. Most doctors are very talented clinicians, yet they shy away from the business and leadership aspects of what they do. They're willing to keep improving on the quality of their service, but they feel uncomfortable improving on the quantity of the people they serve. That doesn't make sense. Part of your reason for becoming a doctor was to help people, and the more people you help, the better off everyone is.

The bottom line is that before you can help people, you need to get them into your office. You cannot serve people until you bring them through the door in the first place. And the way you bring them through the door—and serve them well, during and after their visit—is through learning about and investing in the business aspect of what you do. In the final chapter, I'll discuss the "Big Five" business layers that come together to give you maximum success: marketing, human capital, financial mastery, space and equipment, and clinical duplication.

Allowing business to play a role in your practice does not make you a bad doctor—it empowers you to serve the highest number of people for the greatest good.

SHIFT 5: DRAW THE LINE BETWEEN BUSINESS AND PERSONAL

Finally, the last mindset shift you need to make before you can grow your practice is to draw a clear line between business and personal ideals.

We all have different experiences, and we all bring our different biases, leanings, and judgments into the workplace. That's a problem, because when it comes to running your practice, the transactions that take place should be neutral, without bias or judgment. It's not your place to decide what your patients should or should not buy based on your personal opinions about money, insurance, time, or anything else.

For example, say your administrative assistant would only go to a doctor if her insurance fully covered it. Based on her own experience, her inclination may be to make sure that every patient has full coverage before she lets them in the door. That mindset needs to change, because she has no right to make that kind of decision for a patient. For all she knows, the patient is rich and doesn't care about his insurance coverage. Cost is not his top concern. He just wants convenience and top-quality care.

When you allow your patients to buy whatever they want to buy without judgment, they will purchase significantly more than you will ever offer them. They have every right to buy what they feel is best for them. Never allow your personal biases to interfere with your business transactions.

MINDFUL GROWTH

When I interview new doctors, they always describe how they want their teams to do something differently. Those doctors are never aware that they've trained the people around them to act the way they do, based on their own flawed mindsets about their practices.

Work toward retraining your mind, and you will lay the foundation for a better business. If something isn't going the way you planned, check in with these five changes: taking responsibility, becoming a "yes" office, abandoning the "something for nothing" attitude, accepting that business needs to play a role in your practice, and ensuring that business and personal views don't mix—and see where you're getting off track. Keep your focus where it belongs, on the one thing you have the most control over in your life—you.

When you get your mindset in place, things change. You no longer have excuses. Instead you have data and results, and that creates the rock-solid groundwork for increasing your patient intake. From here, you're ready to take the first step toward actually bringing in new patients: figuring out where you are and establishing a baseline.

CHAPTER 3
CREATE YOUR BASELINE

"Jay, I did everything you said, and it's not working."

I had heard those words before. This time, they were coming from Dr. Scott Grayson, but they always meant the same thing. Somewhere along the line, they had changed part of the plan.

I settled in for a long phone call to figure out what Scott had changed. "Okay," I said to Scott, "tell me everything you've done so far."

After twenty or thirty minutes of relentless digging, I found it. Scott had set his baseline wrong. He was averaging thirteen new patients a month, and instead of targeting a new baseline number of sixteen in accordance with my guidelines, he had set the number at twenty-one. "Sixteen isn't enough," he rationalized at the other end of the line. "I need twenty-one new patients."

"Let me talk to Shelly," I told him. Shelly was the team member who ran Scott's front desk.

Scott put Shelly on the line. "Shelly," I asked, "do you feel like you can get twenty-one new patients? Does that seem possible to you?" She admitted that that number felt out of reach. "Do you think you could get sixteen new patients?" I tried again.

"Yes," Shelly agreed. "That sounds doable."

"Great," I said and had her put Scott back on the line.

"Okay Scott, listen," I told him, "I can get you to twenty-one new patients a month. But you have to give me five months to do it, all right?" Scott agreed, and we took the baseline number down from twenty-one to sixteen.

The next month, Shelly got seventeen new patients. And the month after that, she got twenty-three.

It didn't even take all five of those months to help Scott reach his goal. All it took was setting a baseline target realistic enough for his team to actually get started.

BASIC GROWTH

Dr. Grayson thought that he could take a parked car and set it on the freeway going sixty miles per hour—without starting the engine first. But cars don't work that way, and neither does your new-patient intake process. The first part of the equation is to get the ball rolling, and you do that by determining two things: your current intake average and your baseline.

Your intake average is the mean number of new patients, per month, who enter your office to receive at least a consultation, regardless of referral source. Your baseline is a number, approximately 10 to 15 percent above that new-patient average, that your team is motivated to reach each month.

Your baseline works hand in hand with your team incentive program and your goals for the practice. I'll cover the latter two concepts in chapters 4 and 5. What you need to know is that in order for those other two parts of the mechanism to work, you must create your baseline correctly.

Why? You can't move forward until you know where you are. If you don't get the data about where you stand to begin with, you won't be able to see any progress you're making, you'll make emotional decisions along the way, and ultimately you'll quit before you get to where you want to go. But if you know your starting point, then you have the data you need to track your milestones as you reach them. You have a framework for you and your team to use to celebrate achievements along the path of growth.

One of the greatest gifts you can give your team is an opportunity to win at something. Creating a baseline is what gives them that opportunity. And once they start to taste success, the excitement over those results will fuel bigger and bigger accomplishments.

This chapter will walk you through the process of creating a strong baseline and steer you around the most common pitfall that doctors make when they set out to transform their patient-intake process.

CREATE YOUR BASELINE

To create your baseline correctly, you need to determine your current average new-patient intake, analyze the data for anomalies, and finally calculate the baseline itself.

DETERMINE YOUR CURRENT AVERAGE

The first step in this process is finding your new-patient average.

To determine your average, pull your new-patient numbers for the last three, six, and twelve months. Then do the math. Divide the number of new patients in the last three months by three, the last six months by six, and the last twelve months by twelve.

Now, analyze those numbers. Are they about the same, or are there large differences between them? If they're about the same, you can just take the mean of all three, and that becomes your average.

If they're significantly different, then weigh in any outside factors. For instance, do you run an orthodontic office that tends to get more new patients in summer, when kids are out of school? Do you live in a seasonal resort town, which explains why there are considerably fewer new patients during the off-peak months? Did you open your office a year ago and have large numbers of new patients in the first three months, compared to the months since?

To account for these fluctuations, you can take a three-month average, a six-month average, and a twelve-month average and average them together. This helps to account for sudden, recent growth and weighs the most recent three months essentially three times within the weighted average. By the end of this process, you should have an accurate average based on what is actually occurring in your business.

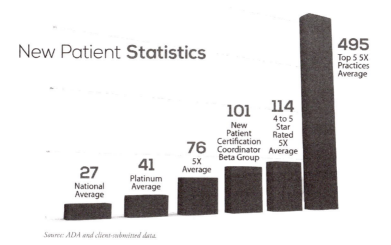

New Patient **Statistics**

495 Top 5 5X Practices Average

114 4 to 5 Star Rated 5X Average

101 New Patient Certification Coordinator Beta Group

76 5X Average

41 Platinum Average

27 National Average

Source: ADA and client-submitted data.

CREATE YOUR BASELINE

Once you know your real average of new patients, you can create your baseline.

First, take your average and increase it by 10 to 15 percent. For example, say you're bringing in an average of ten new patients per month. Using the 10 to 15 percent rule, your result is one to one and a half new patients—always round up. Add those two new patients to your average, and your baseline would be twelve new patients.

Then factor in common sense. If you're dealing with small new-patient numbers, like the ones in this example, you can increase the percentage a little bit. The key element here is that your baseline number needs to look believable. In this case, I can nudge my baseline up to thirteen from twelve, and that still feels very possible.

Be careful not to overdo it. The best way to check whether your baseline is on track is to ask the magic question: If I present the difference between the average and the baseline to my team, will they think the new number is possible to accomplish? The answer to that question should always be a clear "yes." If it's not, you've increased your baseline too much.

Once you've identified your baseline, don't keep revising it. Keep it the same as long as possible. That allows your staff to participate in the consistent growth of the practice, which brings you better results in the long run. Again, I'll explain more about staff incentives in the next chapter.

Finally, you need to take note of the parameters you use as you go through the process of figuring out your average and setting your baseline. You're going to be reanalyzing these numbers again in the future, and that means you need to have clear standards for how you do your analysis if you intend to collect accurate data.

Set up a system for how you want to pull and analyze your data. Create a clear definition of what a "new patient" is in your office. Is a new patient anyone who walks in for a consultation, or is it someone who begins treatment? I usually recommend the former because, most of the time, the people who get consultations will stay. Whichever way you decide to go, make sure that you're consistent.

Work out a process that works for you. Then stick to it as you move forward.

DON'T GET GREEDY

I always include this warning when I teach doctors to calculate their baselines: don't get greedy.

Remember that your baseline is not your ultimate goal for how many new patients you want to bring in. Most doctors make the mistake of setting their baseline number way too high and get no results whatsoever. Your baseline is about starting the engine. That's all. In chapter 5, I'll show you how to get the number of new patients you really want by setting goals. But that comes later. Right now, you cannot skip this basic step.

You have to stay aware of your staff's psychological threshold. Your team won't always tell you if they feel like the baseline you've set is unrealistic. Instead, like Shelly in Dr. Johnson's office, they'll just keep quiet and never even begin to participate in the process.

But if you keep that baseline number within reach, your team will be encouraged by their success, and they'll keep working at improving on it. Most of the time, the results will surpass your expectations. I see this happen all the time.

Never sabotage your ability to produce results by pushing your baseline too high. If you handle this part of the process right, you will set yourself up for the success you want—and then some.

STEADY ON

The most common characteristic of failure is not celebrating progress. You and your team need to feel like you're moving forward. As long as you figure out where you're starting from and set a realistic baseline for progress, you will always be able to celebrate how far you've come, and you will have the motivation to stay the course for the long-term commitment ahead of you.

With a clear idea of where you stand, you're ready to begin the process of actually bringing in new patients. Your team is the key factor in that equation. In the next chapter, I'll show you how to create a strong incentive program for your staff that will put everyone on the same page and propel you in the direction of rapid new-patient growth.

CHAPTER 4

TRAIN YOUR TEAM

When I first started the Scheduling Institute, I used to go into individual offices to help dentists who had bought a day of my time. One of the first practices I visited belonged to Dr. Pete Anderson.

As soon as I walked into his office—before I could even present the system—his front-desk person, Laura, pulled me aside. "Jay," she whispered in my ear, "he needs you. But I want you to know something. I don't have time to do anything extra."

The next practice I went to, the front-desk person said the same thing and then again at the one after that and the one after that. I realized that nothing was going to work if I didn't have the person at the front desk on board. So I came up with an idea.

A few days later, I went back to Dr. Anderson's office and walked straight up to Laura.

"Listen, before we get started, I want to ask you something," I said. "If I could find a way for you to earn a couple hundred extra dollars a month with this system, would you be interested?"

Laura looked right at me and said, "I'll do anything you need me to do."

As soon as she understood that something was in it for her, Laura's issue of being too busy completely disappeared. She willingly pitched in to the program, and Dr. Anderson's practice doubled in a matter of months.

I had found the key to front-desk cooperation: an incentive program.

THE FRONT-DESK FACTOR

The incentive program is a core element of the Scheduling Institute's team training, but it's not the only thing you need to consider. Patients don't call offices just to have a conversation. They call because they're interested in services and want appointments. However, when they call in, the process they encounter doesn't always facilitate those expectations. Many times, the process actually slows them down, makes them question their intentions, or disqualifies them in advance.

The purpose of training your team is to change that paradigm. Your team is everyone who works in your office, including you. We get into the function of each specific team member's role at our on-site training sessions. But, for the purpose of increasing new patients, in this book I'm going to concentrate primarily on the people who actually pick up the telephone and schedule those new patients: the people at your front desk.

When you train your front-desk people, the goal is to teach them how to get the patient across the threshold of your office. This involves showing the team member how to eliminate any barriers that may cause the prospective patient not to schedule the appointment, as well as motivating the team member to participate in the new-patient program to begin with.

Right now, your front-desk people are reactive to calls rather than intentional with them. They're focused on administrative duties instead of generating new patients. When you reverse that focus, it will completely change your new-patient outcomes. Your new-patient intake will typically go up and, in some cases, as much as double with little to no additional marketing dollars needed. If you fail to train your front-desk staff correctly, you will never know how many new patients you're missing.

In this chapter, I'll show you how to make your front-desk people intentional—how to make them proactive instead of reactive—by combining your baseline with incentive and purpose.

HOW TO TRAIN YOUR TEAM

Training your front-desk team members correctly involves presenting the target and incentives, tracking new patients, and certifying your staff.

PRESENT THE TARGET AND INCENTIVES
AND TRACK NEW PATIENTS

The first part of training is simple: show your staff where you are and where you want to go. Use the numbers you calculated in chapter 3: your current average number of new patients and your target baseline. You should also present your ideal goal for new patients, which I'll talk about in the next chapter. Finally, explain the element that makes the whole system work: the incentive program.

The incentive program works like this. First, you assign a dollar amount per new patient; we typically use either five or ten dollars per patient as our guideline. Then, let your team members know that the incentives will kick in at the baseline. That baseline is the magic number. It's the minimum standard to begin receiving additional performance compensation.

Compensation works retroactively down the list of new patients, once the front-desk staff member meets the baseline requirement. In addition, the staff member also receives that same five- or ten-dollar amount for each new patient he or she schedules on top of the baseline number. The incentive program then resets itself each month.

For example, say your baseline number is thirteen, and you're offering a ten-dollar incentive program to your front-desk person, Joni. When Joni schedules her thirteenth new patient of the month, she receives ten dollars for each of the thirteen people on that list—$130 total. Then, if she schedules another new patient, she gets ten more dollars on top of that, bringing her total to $140, and so on with each new patient moving forward. At the end of the month, the new-patient count resets to zero, and she does it all over again.

Creating an incentive program deals with the common staff issues of noncompliance, disinterest, or "I just don't have time." It is the key to making the entire process work. Without it, your front-desk staff will take the same attitude as Laura from Dr. Anderson's office: they'll agree that the practice needs to change, but they themselves will want to stay exactly the same. And if they stay the same, then so will your new-patient numbers.

I mentioned in the previous chapter that once you identify your baseline number, you should keep it steady. The reason for that is because as long as it stays very achievable, your front-desk person will achieve that new-patient number each month. In this way, you can almost guarantee yourself that baseline number of new patients on a recurring basis.

Finally, after you have this system up and running, you should track your new-patient number each month in a way your staff can readily see. I'll explain more about tracking progress in chapter 6.

CERTIFY YOUR STAFF

You can give your team great training, but there's always a difference between the training and what the team members actually do. Many times, your staff will regress to their old habits after the training is over. Training without accountability is just entertainment. To stop that from happening, I recommend certifying your staff on a regular basis.

The certification system we use at the Scheduling Institute is called the 5-Star Challenge. We call the office in question and rate the responses of the person who picks up the phone based on five specific criteria: the greeting, how questions are answered, the transition to the close, the close itself, and data capture.

If the front-desk person checks out with a four- or five-star performance based on these categories, you're in good shape. If the rating is anything lower, it's time to review the training protocol.

Certification is something that has to be maintained. I've seen people be a five-star one day and a one-star the next. We always say, "You're only as good as your last call rating." To really achieve consistency, I usually recommend that my clients get monthly certification calls for each of their front-desk team members.

When you put this training and certification process in place, you will see a huge mental shift in your front-desk people, from reactive mode to intentional mode. And you'll get incredible new-patient results to go along with it.

YOU CAN LEARN MORE ABOUT
THE SCHEDULING INSTITUTE'S
5-STAR CHALLENGE AT
WWW.JAYGEIER.COM

MAKE TOUGH DECISIONS

Your team members will have one of two responses to training. The first response is an immediate increase in performance. The second response is resistance.

Resistance is a very common showdown that occurs in an office implementing change, even before training starts. When you find yourself in a situation where your staff resists training, sometimes you have to make tough decisions as far as whether people stay or leave for the greater good of the practice.

This isn't to say that you need to fire everyone who doesn't immediately jump onboard with training. Many great team members resist training before they embrace it. The important thing is your response as the doctor. The biggest strategic mistake you'll ever make is allowing your staff to determine their own training course. When your team puts up resistance, you cannot allow noncompliance to stand. The only acceptable response to resistance is to not accept it and keep pushing forward.

One client of mine had been working with the same staff member at the front desk for fifteen years, and his practice was bringing in less money than he needed to pay the bills. When he introduced my training program, his staff member put her foot down and said, "I'm not going to do it." So he called me and told me what was going on.

"Okay," I said, "let's look at this in a different way. Your practice is struggling. I know you respect your staff member, but you hired me to help you. I've made many millionaires in the past fifteen years, and during that same span of time, she's made one struggling dentist—you. Just based on the track record, if you let her win on this, what's going to happen?"

It dawned on my client that I was right, so he went back to that team member and said, "Look, you're going to have to do it Jay's way." And even though she resisted at first, once he put his foot down, she actually accepted the training and went on to become really good at her job. This is just one example of a case where the doctor's response was ultimately what made the difference for the success of his practice.

Occasionally you will have a situation where a team member simply refuses to accept the training, and you do need to make the tough decision to let that person go. To make that decision as clean and unemotional as possible for both you and your staff, the Scheduling Institute recommends setting a simple benchmark: staff members need to get certified by a certain date. That's the bottom line. Anyone who is unable to reach certification should find another place to work.

The staff members you want to work with in the long run will have no problem getting certified, because they'll be high-performers. Low-performers resist accountability, make excuses, and create confusion. High-performers love accountability and respond to change in a favorable way.

You should always give each person on your team every chance to get certified and support them in any way you can. But remember that you are the deciding factor. If someone ultimately resists certification, you cannot back down. That is the beginning of regaining control over your team.

ALL FOR ONE

The difference between a job and a career is making an impact. Thousands of people man the front desks of health care practices around the world. When those people are able to bring new patients into the practice, they're also significantly raising the value of what they do. And when people raise the value of what they do, they also raise their self-confidence and feel better about their jobs and lives.

For many years, the Scheduling Institute only offered staff training through our self-study kit. But over time, we discovered that this method robbed the staff members of an experience. When we created our live training program, we found that allowing your staff members to take an entire day to really connect with the purpose and the mission of what they're learning dramatically outperformed the concept of self-study. We've been in over fifteen thousand offices to do on-site trainings and implement it for them. Also, our data shows that within the first ninety days of starting our program, a self-study has a 14 percent average increase while an on-site has an average 46 percent increase.

Average Increase in New Patients For **Self-Study Materials** vs. **On-Site Solution Buyers** in the First 90 Days...

46%

14%

Self-Implementation   On-Site Solution

TO LEARN HOW YOU CAN SEE RESULTS LIKE THESE, VISIT
WWW.JAYGEIER.COM

Once your team is trained and your process for new-patient intake is in place, the mechanism that generates basic, steady growth for your practice is in place. But you don't have to stop at basic growth. In the next chapter, I'll show you how to set effective goals to push your new-patient numbers even higher.

CHAPTER 5
SET GOALS

D r. Josh White and his wife came into my office one day for a private coaching session. As we talked about their practice, the fact that they leased their space came up.

The Whites were in their thirties. "You know," I said, "you guys are very young. I'd really recommend that you buy your own building."

Josh looked right at me and said, "No buildings are available."

"Do you *want* to buy a building?" I asked.

"No buildings are available," Josh repeated bluntly.

I sat back in my chair. "Okay," I said. I explained why buying a building was a good idea for them—they could pay it off over time and it would become a great asset. "So knowing that," I went on, "I don't think the problem is that no buildings are available. I think you don't *want* to buy a building. Tell me you want to buy a building."

Josh looked at this wife, and she looked back at him. Then the two of them looked at me and said, "We're buying a building."

Five days later, Josh called me.

"Well," I said, "did you find any buildings?"

"We're buying the building that we're in," Josh told me.

The Whites had been running their practice from that office for ten years. Before they set their goal to buy a building, they hadn't even seen that the building they were leasing was for sale.

Goals reveal opportunities that already exist—and that's not all they can do.

GO FOR THE GOALS

Most doctors don't set goals at all, and when they do, they go about goal-setting completely wrong. They're fairly conservative, particularly when it comes to risk, so they set goals based on what they think they can accomplish or obtain. That's where the problem begins, because things you already know you can do are not goals.

Goals are ideal outcomes that you would have in an ideal world. They're things that you have never accomplished before. A goal is designed to be a stretch. It's designed to be unattainable—at first.

You set your goals to be a stretch for a reason. If you only set goals based on what you can obtain, you won't grow. Not only will your office be stagnant, it will also encourage loss of control, excuses, low energy, and lack of engagement and learning. But if you set goals right and encourage the right mindset, you will shift the general focus from problems to solutions, empower people to produce results, and create an opportunity for you and your team to win at something.

Good goal-setting is about doing something you've never done before. It's about engaging the next level of your potential by opening your eyes and ears to what's needed to accomplish the goal. When you're just starting out with the program, a goal of increasing new patients by 10 to 15 percent is a good place to start; it doesn't require you to make a lot of changes initially. But over time, raising your goal to doubling your new-patient intake is going to push you to significantly change the way you run your practice.

Practices that are not patient-centric rarely have goals. Practices that are active, vibrant, and full of energy are fueled by goals. You want to belong to the latter category.

This chapter will teach you the fundamentals of goal-setting and show you how to set effective goals for you and your team members.

FUNDAMENTALS OF GOAL-SETTING

Effective goal-setting has four key principles: write it down, be specific, make a plan, and prepare to "fail."

All things start as thoughts, and goals are no exception. The Unity Ministry says that "thoughts held in mind produce after their kind."[1] The easiest and most effective way to keep your goal "held in mind" is to write it down. When you write your goal down on paper, it becomes real in a way that it wasn't before, and that makes it something you can actually pursue. You can also say your goals out loud or post them in public places to keep yourself focused on achieving them.

The next principle of goal-setting is that your goals have to be specific. Everyone in the world wants to do better, but "better" is not specific. The world doesn't respond to "better"; it responds to specificity. Therefore, when you write down your goals, be very clear about what you want, and use benchmarks that can be measured—such as numbers, deadlines, and dates.

After specificity, the third principle of goal-setting is that you need to pair your goal with a matching plan. Plans are what move you and your practice forward. You need to put a plan in place that produces the results you want—goals and plans go hand in hand. People with goals always have plans.

Finally, the fourth and most difficult part of setting effective goals is that you need to be prepared to fail. That is the challenge that keeps most people from following this

---

1   Arturo Mora, "Healthy Thoughts, Healthy Bodies," Unity Worldwide Ministries, http://www.unity.org/sites/unity.org/files/pdf/May2012.pdf.

process correctly. You set your goals to be higher than you think you can reach on purpose—that gives you something to strive for. But because goals are often set so high, most experience failure between the time they're set and the time they're obtained. The majority of people have a habit of setting a goal, not accomplishing it, and then quitting.

You have to reprogram yourself not to fall into the trap of that habit. Most humans don't have a lot of tolerance for failure. They function as if they're being graded on an A/B/C/D scale, and they never want to get a C or a D. But for goal-setting to be effective, you have to learn to tolerate failure for a period of time.

Great goal-setters realize that Bs and Ds are what get them to As over time. They realize that there really is no grading system and that risking failure is just part of the process.

Your goals aren't meant to help you play it safe. That's what your baseline is for. Your goals are meant to take you somewhere you've never been before. You must work hard to accomplish them, and you must be willing to make mistakes along the way.

How do you cope with failure? You train your brain to immediately ask this question: "What do I need to do differently?" Learn the lessons that your failures are there to teach you. Every time you don't hit your goal, that's a sign you need to change something. The trick is looking for the lesson. When you ask yourself what you need to do differently, you'll eventually see the answer—even if you have to ask the question multiple times. Develop your persistence. You just have to keep at it until you get it right.

For example, say you set a goal for your practice to bring in $100,000 by the end of the month, but once the month is over, you find you've only done $50,000. At that point, most people just give up. But you don't. Instead, you ask yourself what you need to do differently and make changes to your process.

Five months later, you hit $100,000 a month, while a person who gave up would still only be bringing in $50,000. And once you learn how to do something one time, it's easy to do it again. The five months you spent "failing" were really your path to success.

Set a goal, and set a timeframe for that goal. If you hit it, set it higher. If you fail, ask yourself what you need to do differently, and then test your new changes, knowing that allowing yourself more time to reach your goal is normal. That is the key to reaching new heights of success in your practice.

SET YOUR OWN GOALS

Goal-setting needs to become part of the culture in your practice, but you can't teach your team to set goals before you learn to set them for yourself. So how do you get started setting your own goals?

The first thing to do is a little self-analysis. What do you want for your practice? Remember to be specific about this: "I want to build this business to *X revenue* and *Y production size* by *Z time*." Look at your own history and see what you've done so far, what you think is doable, and finally what lies beyond that. Then follow the other principles of goal-setting to put yourself on track: write your goals down, make a plan for how to get there, and persist if you don't get what you're aiming for by the set time.

I discovered the value of writing down goals and of persistence through a ten-year experiment I conducted using my own goals. For ten years, I wrote down five goals for eight different areas of my life. I sent those goals to twenty different people who represented a cross-section of the different areas of my life. By writing down my goals, I was achieving 75 to 80 percent of them, and those that I did not achieve the first year were rolling over to subsequent years.

In the first few years, many of the people I sent the lists to read them and shared them with their spouses, and some even decided to write their own lists and share them with me. But after a few years, I discovered, few of the lists were being shared, and no one was sending me their goals anymore. They quit sharing them because they didn't want their spouses to know how much progress I was making based on my lists, and they quit setting their own goals because they didn't want to write down anything they couldn't achieve. That's the difference between good goal-setters and people who sabotage the process. Good goal-setters put the goal in writing and don't give up if they fall a bit short in the planned timeline.

Goals tend to thrive more in group settings than they do in isolation. For instance, at the Scheduling Institute, we find that the people in our coaching program see greater success with their goals just from being around other people who are doing the same thing. That goes hand in hand with getting accountability for yourself. I'll discuss the accountability factor in greater depth in the next chapter.

HELP YOUR TEAM SET GOALS

Once your personal goals are set, you need to help your team set specific goals.

Just like most doctors, most staff members have zero to no training in goal-setting. Because of that, they're losing out on a large part of their potential. Training them to set goals in the workplace is therefore one of the greatest gifts you can give them, not just because of what it accomplishes in the office but because they can take that same skill and transfer it to their personal lives as well.

Many doctors make the major mistake of setting one big goal for the whole team and then neglecting to break it down into smaller units. If you have seven team members, each of those individuals should have a goal pertaining to something they have control over. Your reward is based on what the entire team does, but the team should be rewarded on individual areas of responsibility.

In the case of new-patient intake, then, let's say you're averaging ten new patients per month. You've already figured out that your baseline is thirteen. That's a steady, workable number that your front-desk person feels comfortable about reaching. On top of that, you and that team member set a stretch goal—in this case, maybe sixteen new patients per month. When you hit that milestone of sixteen new patients, you reward that staff member for a job well done. Then you push the target goal even higher.

When you train your team members to set goals and take responsibility for the specific part of the practice they have control over, you will end up with substantially greater results, and everyone will benefit.

GROW YOUR GOALS

Goal-setting never ends. Once you eventually accomplish a goal, that goal becomes your new norm, and it's time to set a new one.

The key to continually growing your practice—and yourself, as a human being—is to constantly reevaluate your goals. That is part of the process of finding and using your God-given potential.

Take a minute to rate yourself on a scale of one to ten on your performance in general. Write down that number. Now,

I want you to rate yourself on a scale of one to ten compared to your God-given potential—what you are capable of. In most cases, your rating on the first example will be pretty high—above average. Then, once given the context of a scale to what your maximum potential is, we often rate ourselves a lot lower. There is a larger upside when you are comparing yourself to your God-given potential than comparing yourself to average.

There are actually no limits to your capabilities. Once you accomplish something, you have to reengage in a new challenge, because what you're really discovering is that your capabilities are now greater than they used to be.

Your goals should always excite you. They should always be something significant. With persistence, you will always get where you want to go eventually, and before long the persistence will become confidence in your track record. The culture of goal-setting will become life-transforming to you, as the doctor, and to your team as well.

Once you master the art of setting goals, your new-patient paradigm shift is almost complete. But there's still one factor left to implement before the system becomes foolproof: tracking and accountability. Chapter 6 will cover this last critical leg in the new-patient intake process.

TRACK YOUR PROGRESS AND GET ACCOUNTABILITY

Y ears ago, I decided to run an accountability test.

I took nineteen clients from all over the country, sat them down, and made them give me the exact incomes of their respective practices, along with their personal incomes. I asked each of them to establish a goal and gave them a series of tips and behaviors to change.

Then I said, "For one year, you are going to be accountable both to me and to each other. You're going to keep track of your progress toward your goals and report it to everyone in this group."

One of the nineteen members was going through a divorce and dropped out because of personal stress. Another left because he just couldn't handle the pressure. But the other seventeen stuck it out. They met in person three times during that year and reported their progress to the others.

By the end of one year, the average increase in business for those group members was 40 percent—and some of them saw significantly higher gains. They were so impressed with their own progress that they kept the group going, and many of them are still Scheduling Institute clients today.

That yearlong test proved to me the importance of tracking and accountability, and those components have been a staple of my programs ever since.

Accountability

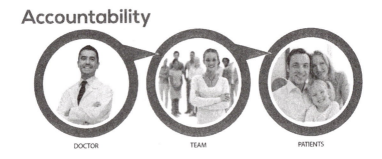

DOCTOR   TEAM   PATIENTS

ACCOUNT FOR PROGRESS

Accountability happens on two levels. You need accountability for your team, and you need it for yourself.

A fundamental form of accountability is *tracking*. One of the basic principles of business is that to make anything increase, you need to track and measure it. The only way to troubleshoot, modify, and adjust is to keep a consistent tracking process in place.

This is especially important in a medical practice, because you're not just a business owner. You're both a doctor and a manager. You have to depend on your specific process to provide clarity about expectations and performance to your staff on a regular basis, because you don't have time to do that yourself. You're always busy doing something else.

The key payoff of tracking is that you and your staff members are attempting to learn how to control your outcomes, instead of letting outside circumstances control you. When you consistently track progress, you inspire forward movement in yourself and your team. If you avoid measurement and accountability altogether, your practice will stagnate.

In this chapter, I'll teach you how to create a powerful tracking system for your team and show you how to set up equally powerful accountability for yourself, as the team leader.

YOUR TEAM TRACKING SYSTEM

The key to tracking and accountability with your team is coming up with a system that makes the staff's priority the same as what you feel is necessary for the business.

Most team members simply want to do what you want them to do; the problem is that you're not providing enough clarity as to what that is. When you create the tracking system for your team, you have to build it around answering that question: What is the core purpose and priority of each person in the office?

Once you get this part right, your staff will not only be as much as 20 to 30 percent more productive but also bring a sense of pride, focus, and momentum to their jobs from having something specific that they own and for which they are responsible.

Building a tracking system for your staff is a six-step process. You must identify a measurable result for each staff member, confirm agreement of ownership, establish the system itself, track progress every day, modify behavior as needed, and celebrate progress.

STEP 1: IDENTIFY A MEASURABLE RESULT

The first step in the process is identifying a specific, measurable result that you want your team members to produce.

I'm not talking about the list of activities that a team member does each day. Most people mistake those activities for their measurable result, which is a big part of the problem. For example, nine times out of ten, when I walk into an office and ask the front-desk person, "What do you do?" he or she will reply, "I answer the telephone and greet patients." That staff member will never say, "I'm in the new-patient business."

That's why you must narrow the list of activities down to the particular result that you want each team member to produce. Each person should know exactly what part of the business's production he or she is responsible for supporting.

In the case of the front desk, new patients are the result you want, so bringing those new patients in should be clearly identified as the primary purpose and priority of the staff member in that role. You could also argue that the front-desk person is in the patient-referral business and the business of scheduling follow-up appointments. However, you never want to assign more than two or three priorities to any particular person, or you risk weakening your results.

When you convert activities into specific, measurable results, you raise the overall productivity of both your team members and yourself.

STEP 2: AGREEMENT OF OWNERSHIP

The second step in creating your team tracking system is establishing agreement of ownership. Once you've identified measurable results for your staff members, it's important that each person accepts responsibility for making it happen.

That mutual acceptance of responsibility is very important—not only for the staff members but also for the doctor or team leader. Many doctors are reluctant to assign responsibility to team members or to a team leader (who would then delegate), because they don't have a guarantee that the staff will achieve the results the doctor wants. Many doctors feel like they have to explain exactly what they want their staff to do all the time.

This is a very fundamental mistake that I see in many offices. Not only is it a waste of your time, it's a waste of the God-given potential that your staff brings to the table. You simply have to give your team members the chance to accept responsibility and see what happens in order for the tracking system to work. If they make mistakes, you can correct them later. The important factor in the equation is empowering your staff to make things work on their own.

It's true that your entire team is connected, and in that respect, everyone is partially responsible for the different results your practice produces. But ultimately, you need to allow each member of the team to be an owner of a certain statistic and be responsible for its impact on the practice. And as the team grows, we recommend that doctors develop leaders in the major areas of their practices, such as a front-desk leader and a clinical leader. This is the best way to track accountability among your staff.

STEP 3: ESTABLISH THE TRACKING
AND ACCOUNTABILITY SYSTEM

After you've laid the foundation by identifying a clear result and agreeing on ownership of it, you can establish the tracking and accountability system itself.

That is usually done by some type of public display—a graph, a chart, or another kind of visual medium. We use daily graphs to show where you are tracking against your baseline.

Making the tracking display public is key. Don't bury team results in a computer somewhere where nobody can see them. Instead, keep the display posted in a break room or another common area where everyone can see it. Keeping the results public creates accountability and raises the level of focus on making daily progress.

STEP 4: TRACK PROGRESS EVERY DAY

Once your public tracking system is up and running, the next step is to use it every day.

A great expression that describes how well this works is, "The only way you eat an elephant is one bite at a time." End goals can be intimidating. Your front-desk person may look at a goal of sixty new patients per month and feel like it's unattainable. But if you break those sixty patients down into just two new patients per day, the impossible suddenly becomes very achievable.

Keeping up with progress day by day usually prevents people from getting behind on their goals. That is an important part of the system, because when people get too far behind, they tend to quit emotionally. If they report progress often and consistently, they have a better chance of staying on track.

Daily tracking has another benefit. At the end of the day, when your team members go to that graph and register their results, it inspires them to adjust their behavior for the following day. If they achieved what they wanted, they'll carry that positive motivation into tomorrow's results. If they fell below the result they wanted, they'll be motivated to make up for it.

The important thing is to track continuously, regardless of whether the results are good or bad. Most people tend to track when they're doing well and stop tracking when they're doing poorly. Not tracking is an avoidance of accountability, and even "bad" results can be turned into positive assets, as I'll explain next.

STEP 5: MODIFY BEHAVIOR AND CREATE A TRACK RECORD

Reporting results of any kind produces something indispensable to your team: a track record.

If you're tracking new patients and have a few days where no results are added to the public display, that's a sign that behavior needs to be adjusted. Your track record helps you figure out what you need to change. Just like you're going to have days where results don't meet your expectations, you're also going to have days where they exceed expectations. You can compare what happened on the good days to what happened on the bad days and adjust the process accordingly.

Modifying behavior is something that takes constant study. However, over time, it will help your team build a tool chest of strategies and habits that they can use to control their results. The key is capturing information nonstop to give your track record as much useful data as possible.

STEP 6: CELEBRATE PROGRESS

The final element in your team's tracking system is celebrating progress.

Learning to celebrate progress is critical to the continued growth of your practice. The majority of people who do not recognize the progress they make don't feel motivated or good about themselves, even if they're moving closer to their goal. By contrast, you can raise the productivity of your practice by 25 percent if your staff members feel like they're "winning" on a regular basis.

There are several ways to celebrate progress. One of them is by rewarding people financially. If you want to get a result from someone on a consistent basis without having to invest an enormous amount of time in it, a financial reward is often the way to go. Handing your staff member that check can be a wonderful celebration. Positive reinforcement, in terms of verbal acknowledgment and appreciation, can also go a long way with your team.

One of the hardest things for doctors to do is celebrate specific areas of progress when other parts of the practice are suffering from different problems. That is a huge mistake, because it stifles the positive momentum you have and makes the rest of your problems even bigger.

Get in the habit of constantly celebrating any kind of improvement in your practice, small or large, instead of focusing on all the things you're not happy about. When you focus on the positive things, your staff will follow your lead—and that will resolve the problems you have faster than worrying about them will.

YOUR PERSONAL ACCOUNTABILITY SYSTEM

Just like you need to establish clear standards for your staff, you need to set up accountability for yourself that motivates you to stay focused on your goals.

Most dentists and many doctors have no accountability, because they own their practices. This is a huge problem; as humans, our brains are very good at justifying things and hiding from accountability. The less accountability we have, the more frustrated we are, the more our businesses decline, and the more we foster bad habits that turn us into excuse-makers. On the other hand, when we agree to accept accountability and behave according to a set standard, we become high-performers who produce extraordinary results.

Your accountability is really everyone around you, including your team and your personal support network. However, the best way to create self-accountability that gets results is to hire a coach, instructor, or topic-specific expert to give you feedback and monitor your progress. You can also join a mastermind group and attend regular meetings to disclose what you've accomplished and what you're attempting to produce. Make a commitment to being exposed to or learning about what is required to achieve your particular objective.

The Scheduling Institute has the largest coaching program in the world tailored specifically for doctors and dentists. We provide coaching services in a number of different ways, and we've created dedicated facilities just for this purpose.

TO LEARN MORE ABOUT
THE SCHEDULING INSTITUTE'S
COACHING PROGRAM, VISIT
WWW.JAYGEIER.COM

MAKE IT COUNT

At the highest levels, the most successful doctors I've coached have created tracking and accountability in every area of their lives, both business and personal. When you give yourself standards to live up to, you'll find that you really do live up to them—and then some. This is what ultimately creates value for you, your patients, and your team.

By the time you reach tracking and accountability, your new-patient intake process will already be in great shape. You will see impressive results in your practice from implementing these strategies alone. But new-patient intake is only the beginning of a much larger journey when it comes to enabling your business to reach its full potential. In the next chapter, I'll show you what to expect on the road ahead as you continue to grow your patient-centric practice.

CHAPTER 7

THE NEXT HORIZON

A dentist by the name of Dr. Max Harris came up to me after a team-building event.

"Jay," he said in a quiet, earnest voice, "I'm really struggling with this team concept. Can I tell you a story?"

"Sure," I said. "Tell me your story."

"When I was in high school, we had a football team," Max began. "Some of the guys on the team used to be physically abusive to me." That was just the start of his story. Max had also been through event after event of physically traumatic experiences from people in the years after high school. "I've had a negative connotation about teams my whole life," he admitted. "I didn't get into dentistry to work with a team. I got into it to *avoid* teams."

He was so authentic, and I did the best I could to support him. "I hear you," I said. "That's a tough story. But try to look at this in a different way. Your redemption is in being a great boss to your team now, not in reserving your potential as a leader because of what people have done to you in the past."

When Max left that day, I wasn't sure if what I'd said had actually affected him or not. But, several months later, the Scheduling Institute ran a video contest—and one of the submissions was from Max.

In that video, Max told his story. His journey was about overcoming barrier after barrier after barrier. More than that, it was a story about a guy who actually began to let the light shine on himself and his practice. He had learned to become comfortable telling people who he was and what he was doing. He had learned to love his team. Best of all, he went on to describe how his family and his business had blossomed as a result of his personal transformation.

His practice had come to life because *he* had come to life.

THE ROAD AHEAD

Growing your practice is like peeling an onion. In this book, we've peeled back the first layer: increasing your new-patient intake through training your front-desk team. But once you get those new patients, you will be faced with new challenges that you didn't anticipate—as well as new opportunities to grow.

I've spent more than twenty years studying the process of growing a medical practice, and I've mapped out what the challenges are. For example, when you raise your new-patient numbers, you also raise your income. And if your income goes up to $500,000 a year, you're going to have different financial needs than a person making $100,000.

You don't know what your new needs are going to be yet, because this is your first experience growing your practice. You're setting goals that energize you and venturing into unknown territory. That's exciting, but it can also be a little scary. The good news is that I've guided so many thousands of doctors through this process that I can forecast what your needs will be, and in this chapter, I want to share with you what the road ahead looks like.

What I've discovered is that there are five major layers when it comes to growing your practice—the "Big Five" that come together to give you maximum success. These five layers are marketing, human capital, space and equipment, financial mastery, and clinical duplication.

LAYER 1: MARKETING

After you correct your new-patient intake process, the next step on the road to growing your practice is marketing.

Marketing is the system or process that allows you to tell people who you are and what you do. There's no reason to put any energy into this area until you have a certified person answering your phones. But once you're ready to move to the next level, marketing is ultimately what drives your business forward. It leads to substantial growth in all areas of the practice.

Marketing has a negative connotation to many doctors; in fact, it wasn't too long ago that marketing was illegal in dentistry. They're worried about how they'll be perceived if they market themselves. But the truth is that your marketing is really a reflection of the confidence you have in your quality of service. If you're not willing to expose or market your services to people, that's actually a direct reflection of how valuable you think your services are. And by the same token, sharing who you are and what you do is the ultimate sign of belief in your system.

The marketing approach we use with our doctors at the Scheduling Institute looks nothing like the one we use to market ourselves. We don't encourage you to market aggressively like we do, because you're running a different kind of business. To most of our clients' surprise, our marketing program is very conservative, internally focused, and extremely low cost. When we add an external process, we make sure it's necessary, and we only implement it after the internal process is working.

TO LEARN MORE ABOUT
THE SCHEDULING INSTITUTE'S
COACHING PROGRAM, VISIT
WWW.JAYGEIER.COM

LAYER 2: HUMAN CAPITAL

After marketing, the next area of your practice to grow is human capital.

Human capital is everything related to the management, development, and inspiration of all human beings associated with your business—including you. This is really about leadership and developing the full, God-given potential of you and the people around you.

It's also the single most difficult principle of the Big Five, to the point where I could almost call human capital the "big one" and the others the "little four." Human capital is complex, and it is lifelong in nature. Most people make the mistake of thinking that there's a start and a finish with human capital, and because that's not the case, they give up on it. The truth is that human capital is never done, because with each new advancement comes new opportunity.

That's what makes it such a powerful factor in your practice. You have a people business. Every experience and interaction with your staff and patients is a mirrored reflection of your commitment to human capital. Your employees will only be as good as your commitment to them in training and development. If you want the highest level of patient experience, you have to match that by investing money, time, and energy in the people who work for you.

All great companies have a huge commitment to developing the people inside the business—and most doctors don't know how dysfunctional their old team was until they get a good one. At the Scheduling Institute, we teach doctors to start investing in human capital, raise engagement, and then pursue this principle for life.

LAYER 3: SPACE AND EQUIPMENT

The fourth member of the Big Five for growing your practice is space and equipment.

Space and equipment are simply the physical assets of where you work. It includes your building, your office, and the contents of the office. When you have the right space and equipment, your net worth goes up, and your business becomes supercharged. Providing the appropriate space and equipment is one of the best things you can do for your practice, as an individual business owner.

However, most doctors don't have the right space and equipment. Instead, they have what I call a "trap." They make the common mistake of buying their space and equipment too small and then keeping them for too long. Doctors don't realize that space and equipment come with built-in limitations in income, and the longer they stay in the wrong building, the less money they'll be able to get out of it. Most people don't know how to diagnose that problem correctly.

Space and equipment are the easiest part of the Big Five to fix. However, most doctors tend to make it into an insurmountable barrier in their minds. Our program at the Scheduling Institute is designed to take you out of the trap you're in and get you into an office that is capable of generating the results you would like to have. We like to turn people into active real estate investors who use their business to pay off their investment over time and leave a legacy for their family.

LAYER 4: FINANCIAL MASTERY

The third principle of the Big Five is financial mastery.

Financial mastery is the lifelong process of improving the quality of your relationship with money and everything associated with it, including decisions, investments, and people. For most people, mastering money reveals their creativity and gives them the resources they need to become what they want to be. Very few people who are struggling financially accomplish things of significance. You need money to realize your full ability to affect people.

The statistics suggest that most people don't master money. When you combine personal finances with business finances, the complexity more than doubles. This is even more complicated for doctors, because they are perceived as rich, but most have a mountain of debt that we have to help get rid of; we focus on net worth overall, not just increasing production.

As your practice grows and becomes more complex, you need to be fully educated on how to improve all areas related to finance, in both your personal and professional life.

LAYER 5: CLINICAL DUPLICATION

Your ability to create new patients is fairly unlimited. However, your ability to personally deliver service to those new patients *is* limited. That's where the last of the Big Five principles enters the picture: clinical duplication.

As your age goes up, the willingness to work declines; and as time goes on, new-patient numbers rise in your practice. Clinical duplication is the solution to this equation. It is the process of training someone else to deliver the service you used to deliver yourself—and it is the ultimate in freedom, because it allows you to increase your income without spending more time in your office.

For doctors or dentists who achieve clinical duplication, the growth opportunities discovered become greater than anything they have ever imagined, and their ability to affect other people multiplies accordingly.

Clinical duplication is often the greatest barrier to growth in a practice. Many doctors spend enormous amounts of time on clinical training, and they create the mental construct for themselves that no one else can do what they do. But when you overcome this hurdle and acknowledge that you do not actually have to be the one to see the patient, running your business actually becomes easier on you, physically.

Every trend in the modern marketplace indicates that this is the single greatest time in the history of dentistry to recruit, train, and hire a dentist to work in your office. In 2014 alone, the Scheduling Institute placed more than three hundred associate dentists in our clients' offices. But just like every other area of the business, one key thing makes that kind of success possible: the doctor's acceptance of responsibility for this final frontier of growth.

ONE STEP AT A TIME

If you try to attack the process of building a practice all at once, in its entirety, it becomes overwhelming. What I suggest, and what I have been doing successfully with thousands of doctors for years, is to take the complicated and turn it into something simple. The best way to do that is as straightforward as it gets: just put one foot in front of the other.

Most people have a tendency to try to think about the consequences of all the steps in the growth process before they take the first one. That creates paralysis. It robs you of all the great possibilities that are lying in wait for you.

So what I encourage my clients to do is to take one step at a time. The first step is your patient-intake process. That is the key to moving forward and creating all the other opportunities that will pertain to your practice later. Have a conversation with us. Let us show you why there is a major problem at the very front of your business. The front desk is ten feet away from the doctor and may be sabotaging the practice, but no one has any idea it's happening.

Don't let yourself worry about what's happened in the past or what's going to happen afterward. Simply allow us to solve just that one thing in your practice. From there, the next step will become clear.

When you're moving into territory you've never seen before, you just have to learn to trust and take the next step upward. Sometimes, the view from there is greater than you ever could have imagined from the step below.

VISIT

WWW.JAYGEIER.COM

AND TAKE THE 5-STAR CHALLENGE
TO DISCOVER EXACTLY HOW YOU
ARE DOING WITH YOUR CURRENT
NEW-PATIENT INTAKE PROCESS.

THE DOOR OF OPPORTUNITY

I have a painting hanging in my office that I commissioned myself. It's a painting of a door with a light behind it, and it's called "The Door of Opportunity." I keep it there as a reminder that every decision I make may be opening up a door and that just thinking about what to do never succeeds in pushing that door open. Only action does.

You may not feel that you are living up to your God-given potential yet, but that opportunity is always there. Right now, you can begin the process of significantly increasing the investments that you make in your development, the development of the people on your team, and the development of your business.

The success stories I've seen come in every shape, size, location, and background imaginable. Many of my clients started out thinking that growing their practices into profitable businesses was beyond them. You probably have all kinds of reasons that make you think you can't succeed, just like they did.

But what if all of those reasons are wrong? Stop for a moment and imagine if that were true. Because it is.

What it takes is turning your practice into a patient-centric one—a business that puts patients first. That is achieved by first changing your mindset—getting your head in the right place. Then you must create a realistic baseline on which to build. You must have a team that is trained and incentivized. You must set specific goals and work toward them—and don't forget to celebrate your successes! Finally, you must monitor your progress and get accountability, both for your team members and for yourself.

The only dangerous thing you can do is not walk through the next door. The journey that you're on—of discovering your God-given potential—never ends. When you come right down to it, this isn't about what you accomplish. It's about the pursuit of your capabilities.

I can't tell you what that pursuit has in store for you. I can only tell you that if you keep pursuing this path, you will always live a life of significance and excitement. You will always unlock greater and more impactful things.

You will always have a bigger door of opportunity to walk through.

INFO@JAYGEIER.COM.

LET US SHOW HOW THE PRINCIPLES, PROCEDURES, PROCESSES, AND SYSTEMS THAT WE TEACH—AND THAT WE EMPLOY OURSELVES—CAN HELP YOUR PRACTICE REACH ITS FULL BUSINESS POTENTIAL.

OUR SERVICES

When your practice is a grind, it's incredibly difficult to care for patients, support your staff, give your family and friends the care and attention they need, and take care of your own personal goals. With our tried-and-true, step-by-step solution, we'll help you transform your practice into a business (not a job) and create the practice and lifestyle you've been dreaming of.

We have an army of support people trained to help you and your team transform your new-patient intake process. Then we'll assist you with the "Big Five," which are the five major areas you should invest in to grow your practice.

marketing

human capital

space and equipment

financial mastery

clinical duplication

The Scheduling Institute
World Headquarters
4125 Old Milton Pkwy • Alpharetta, GA 30005

info@JayGeier.com

*For more information on Jay Geier and to learn how he can help your practice, visit **JayGeier.com**.*